WISLEY HANDBOOK 43

Gardening by the Sea

F. W. Shepherd

LONDON
The Royal Horticultural Society
1982

Contents

Acknowledgements:

Black and white photographs supplied by Pat Brindley and the Harry Smith collection.

The map on page 21 is reproduced from *Climatological Memorandum No. 73* by permission of the Controller, Her Majesty's Stationery Office.

Introduction

To those who have visited the seaside, and who has not, gardening by the sea may bring to mind bright displays of spring bulbs or summer bedding in luscious gardens under the control of the local parks department. Others will remember windswept trees and shrubs with sometimes unfamiliar plants crouching in their lee. But those who have the good fortune to live and garden near the sea will know that the brilliant bedding displays are rarely possible for them, because time and money are not available for the production of the plants and the clearing and replanting of the beds, and because such displays must be in a sheltered dell or they run the risk of being damaged beyond recovery in a sudden gale. Those with such experience know that the windswept tree must be the hallmark of their gardening.

The many who think of retiring to a seaside town or village and who wish to start or continue gardening as their hobby must appreciate that they will enter a new phase in their gardening experience. In addition to the new problems they will face in their gardens there will still be the old ones. Weeds, sometimes different ones, continue to grow; diseases and pests still appear; mowing and pruning still need attention. To some the distractions and competition of other hobbies, particularly sailing or fishing, will reduce the time for gardening and their hobby may fade a little.

This booklet sets out to tell of the differences between seaside gardening and inland gardening, to explain the difficulties and assist in overcoming these problems. We will limit our scope to those situations that are within the reach of onshore winds that carry salt and, in some cases, sand from the shore.

Against the problems and distractions of seaside gardening there are advantages that the new seaside gardener should not forget. He can take heart that there are many plants new to him that thrive in very windy situations; that the pleasure of a sheltered garden or part of a garden near the sea is increased both by the physical relief it can give to the gardener and the joy of undamaged plants that thrive when wind is excluded. There are also the many plants that in inland Britain are rare except in greenhouses, but can be grown in the milder climates. Of the differences in seaside gardening, the climatic factors, of immoderate winds, but more moderate temperatures, are the most important. Let us turn first to the wind.

Wind

The most important feature of the seaside climate is undoubtedly the wind. It is stronger when coming in over the uninterrupted surface of the sea and it picks up salt spume from the waves and, in some places, fine sand from the shore to add to its damaging abilities.

Winds may bend, break, scorch, tear and uproot many plants unused to its effects and some of this damage is increased when salt and sand are included in the assault. Many good garden plants of inland areas are unused to such attacks and suffer accordingly, but from the sea coasts of many countries have come plants that survive and even thrive in the presence of wind, salt and blown sand. We will return to them later, but it is to them that we must turn both for protection for more common garden plants and as the chief inhabitants of exposed gardens.

Wind also reduces temperature so a sheltered garden is a milder garden although, particularly in winter, sea winds bring slightly warmer air which has been in contact with the sea with its higher temperatures rather than the cold winter earth.

Damage caused by wind allows fungus diseases to enter and spread more readily in the plant. The spores of some fungi causing plant diseases can only enter the cultivated plant through damaged tissue and such damage is often to be found on leaves and branches, flowers and fruit that have been exposed to sea winds. At the same time the moister atmosphere by the sea also improves the conditions in which many disease fungi thrive.

It must not be thought that winds only flow onshore or from one direction. Even with the so-called prevailing winds it is rare that more than 40% of the wind comes annually from one of the four quarters of the compass or more than 25% from the southwest, usually the source of the strongest and most frequent winds. Strong winds can and do come from all quarters and when from overland may cause less damage than the salt laden sea winds but, in winter, when from north or east, they may carry snow and frost that are equally damaging.

The wind-shaped thorns or other trees may suggest long periods of strong gales from off the sea but the shaping is not the result of persistent winds. It is nearly always the result of pruning by the wind, perhaps only once a year, when really strong salt-laden gales kill or shorten all new growth directly exposed to it. After such wind-pruning the unexposed twigs and branches will continue to grow to leeward and the well-known leaning tree will develop.

On the east coast the onshore winds are, in winter, the cold winds; so protection from their several damaging effects is even more important. The farther south and west one goes the less important will be the freezing effects of onshore winds. Salt damage will occur but protection will be needed against those from other quarters unless the garden is protected by a hill or woodlands on the landward side.

Shelter

Before looking at the means of providing shelter let us consider the effect of barriers on windspeed and direction. Wind cannot be stopped, but it can be deflected and filtered. A solid barrier deflects it and when this happens the speed increases at the top or ends of the barrier. This is often to be noticed at street corners or between two solid hedges where the wind is deflected and the air whistles round or through at greater speeds.

Immediately behind a solid barrier, there will be an area of comparative calm but farther away the wind drives downwards from the high pressure area cancelling the deflection. Thus in the lee of solid windbreaks some shelter can be found but then there will be an area of turbulence and wind eddying where damage may be caused to plants.

Permeable barriers, from a moderately thick hedge to wire netting, allow some wind to pass through at reduced speeds but send some of it over the top or around the ends as with a solid wall. It will be obvious that wire netting will reduce the speed only a little whereas a thickish hedge will reduce speeds considerably but may cause wind eddying to leeward.

The optimum permeability for a shelter is about 60% solid to 40% apertures. This considerably reduces wind speeds and causes little turbulence. The lath fences once widely used to protect west country flower fields and still available in a few places, are near this optimum degree of permeability. The laths are one inch wide and spaced one inch apart. These, plus the cross timbers on which they are mounted and the broad bracing diagonals, produce this pattern of 60 : 40.

The diagrams on page 6 illustrate the wind patterns when blowing against permeable shelter trellis, screens or hedges. It must be remembered that they are somewhat simplified diagrams and that each situation will be different and may produce areas of exposure or shelter that need study on the ground in order to explain them and take account of them.

Quite simply a solid barrier will give good shelter up to 2H (twice the height of the barrier) and there will then be an area of turbulence up to 7H away. A barrier of 60 : 40 permeability will produce little turbulence and will reduce wind speed at ground level as shown in the diagrams, up to a distance of about twenty times its height, but with the maximum protection only within about 5H.

Armed with this knowledge of the effect of shelter on wind and bearing in mind the necessity of good shelter for all seaside gardens how do we set about providing it? As always each situation will need special attention. Depending on the size, the aspect, surrounding shelter and the wishes of the gardener, a large garden will probably need tall shelter belts of suitable trees. In smaller gardens living hedges or artificial windbreaks are needed.

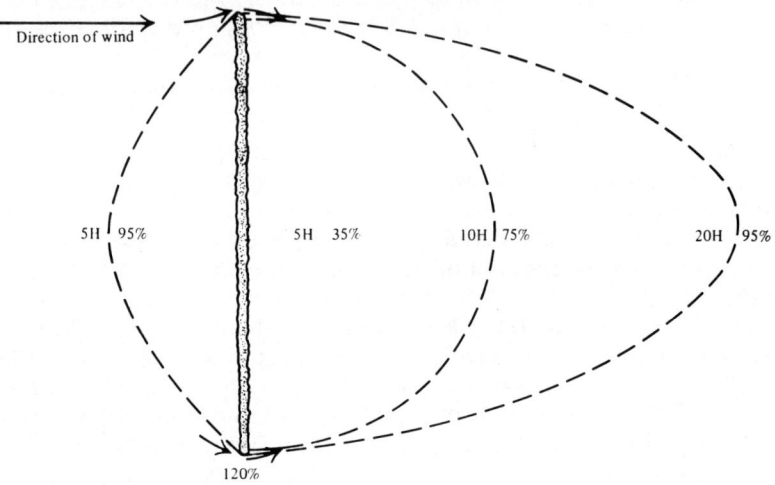

Direction of wind

95%	85%	hedge	35%	75%	95%
5H	2H		5H	10H	20H

a Cross section, to scale, of hedge standing at right angles to direction of wind, showing percentages of original wind speeds at various distances in heights of hedge to windward and leeward of hedge. Measurements at ground level.

Direction of wind

5H 95%   5H   35%   10H 75%   20H 95%

120%

b Plan to illustrate effect of a relatively short length of hedge on wind speeds. Figures in percentages of original wind speed measured at more than 10H to windward or 30H to leeward of any shelter.

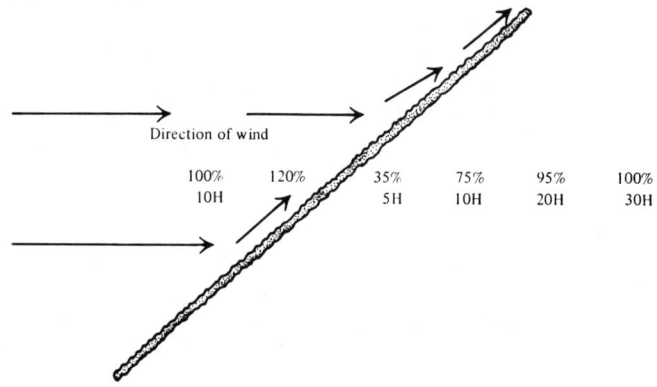

Direction of wind

100%	120%	35%	75%	95%	100%
10H		5H	10H	20H	30H

c Plan of ground surrounding a hedge with wind blowing at an angle of 45° to it, showing percentages of original wind speeds in relation to the hedge. Measurements of wind speeds taken along line of original direction of wind and not at right angles to hedge.

In almost every case the gardener will want a view of the sea, if possible. To allow this a series of low screens on the seaward side of the ground will provide useful shelter for smaller plants and allow the view to be enjoyed over their tops. If the gardener is prepared to wait for a year or two living hedges are preferable to artificial ones. The 'instant' gardener will want artificial fences and screens.

Shelter belts

These may be defined as two or more rows of trees, unpruned and growing to their full height and spread. Three rows are often recommended and even wider belts have been planted in exposed country but they are often for the protection of livestock and the possible production of timber and two rows of suitable trees will suffice for most garden purposes.

Well spaced mature trees will provide permeable shelter and good protection to plants growing in their lee. Thus, when 50 feet (15m) high ground up to 250 feet (76m) away can be well protected and there will be some reduction in wind speed up to 1,000 feet away (300m).

These trees do take time to grow and we cannot afford the time allowed by Osgood Mackenzie at Inverewe in the north of Scotland who planted *Pinus radiata* and then left it for over 25 years! Useful shelter will, however, be provided by such a belt of trees within 10 years, but meanwhile inner shelter can be provided by temporary artificial shelter or quick growing hedges. They can be removed as the shelter belts become effective.

All trees for shelter belts or for any other purpose in windy situations are best planted as young seedlings. They are often described as 1×1 in catalogues, which means that they have had one year in the seed bed and one year lined out before being lifted for planting in their permanent positions. Such plants have the opportunity of making a good root system before the top becomes too large. Older, larger, trees have too much top growth and too little root and are thus likely to be blown over by strong winds. Staking is expensive and often useless in windy situations. Such tree seedlings will benefit from early protection while forming their roots and really need protection from smothering, if not competing, weeds.

The young trees in their two rows are best planted as 'staggered' rows and not opposite each other and, for many species, 6 feet (1.8m) each way is a suitable distance. Thorough cultivation and the elimination of perennial weeds in a strip of land 12 feet (3.6m) wide is good preparation for a two row shelter belt. After planting application of a residual herbicide (such as simazine) between but not on the seedling trees will permit a good start to be made, without competition from weeds. There should be no further cultivation because roots may be damaged and loosening the soil may allow the young trees to be blown over more easily.

7

Sowing grass between the trees will assist the soil to settle and hold the roots firmly in place. It should not be sown right up to the trunk, but a circle about 2 feet (60cm) in diameter should be left clear. It can be kept cut to reduce competing weeds and another application of a weedkilling chemical (such as simazine) around the young trees in the second spring after planting, will keep the grass and weeds away from them. It must be noted that the common garden weeds, mainly annuals, are of no great harm to growing trees. It is brambles, elder, thorn and larger trees such as ash and sycamore that are most likely to spoil a shelter belt.

The choice of trees to form shelter belts by the sea is limited. As with so many choices in gardening, a careful study of neighbouring plantings and a word with those who garden or have nurseries in similar situations will greatly assist in making a choice. The most effective are evergreens which give protection all the year round.

Pinus radiata. In the south and west this quick growing, massive tree from the western North American seaboard is as good as any. Singed by the heaviest spray but remaining upright and firm at the roots it grows two or more feet each year after it is established.

Pinus contorta. This species is from a wider range of conditions on and west of the Rockies and the hardier forms may be more suitable in colder districts here.

Cupressus macrocarpa. When close clipped as a hedge this North American tree is a great disappointment but when allowed to grow untouched in the milder districts it is one of the toughest of all seaside trees.

Quercus ilex. This, the European evergreen oak, is slower growing than the three conifers already mentioned but is just as stable and longer lived. It is distinctive in both form and growth.

All these four are best thinned as they grow, first to 12 feet (3.6m) apart and even further if growth is good. This will allow them to spread and make the massive trees that stand and give their shelter so well.

× *Cupressocyparis leylandii.* This hybrid tree has been widely planted and somewhat maligned for its instability. Like the others it must be young when planted. One year cuttings grown on in pots and not grown on for longer periods in other containers and therefore with unrestricted roots, are best. The soil, particularly for this plant but for all others, must be deep enough to allow vigorous root growth. Shallow soils over chalk or rock close to the surface will prevent deep rooting and the rapidly growing tops will have insufficient anchorage.

Ash *(Fraxinus excelsior)* and sycamore *(Acer pseudoplatanus)* will provide some protection on exposed sites but will always be wind-shaped near the coast and always, therefore, less effective than the others. The loss of their leaves in winter will also reduce their efficiency as shelter, but this may not always be a disadvantage if the plants being sheltered are only susceptible in the summer. There may be some advantages as the

Fig. 1. Pinus contorta, a good species for use as a shelter belt.

leafless trees allow more light into the sheltered area.

Problems frequently facing those who own older seaside gardens are firstly the thinning of tree bottoms and, then, the loss of trees as they reach maturity and branches or the whole tree cannot withstand a particularly strong gale.

Where the bottom of the shelter belt has thinned out the planting of one of the shrubs suggested below will fill such gaps. If there is space plant on the windward side, if not on the lee of the shelter belt or on the sunny side if possible. Planting between the rows is rarely successful because there is too much root competition in the soil and too little light above.

In the later life of a shelter belt the loss of a single tree may be serious. The wind will rush at increased speeds through the gap left and any replacement will certainly need local protection if it is to make any headway.

Outer screens
In the teeth of the wind, on the shore or a cliff edge, any rough vegetation will be a welcome protection for newly planted shelter belts or hedges. Native gorse, elder, sycamore, sea buckthorn, ash and quickthorn may be planted or, with the inevitable brambles, left to grow on the windward side of more formal plantings. They will all be singed and battered but will provide some protection for young trees or shrubs while they become established and start to form shelter belt or hedge. They will later prove the point that there is some reduction in wind speed on the windward side of windbreaks as they grow taller as the plants in their lee grow taller.

If it can be established, the New Zealand flax, *Phormium tenax* will stand boldly in such exposed positions. So also will some bamboos, particularly *Arundinaria japonica*. They will look tattered and bedraggled after severe gales but will send up new growths each spring that will give some shelter to other plants. Bamboos are particularly good in moist rich soils.

Hedges
A single row of plants, trimmed to a predetermined height and breadth forms a formal hedge; a single row of shrubs permitted to grow almost untrimmed will form an informal hedge.

Almost any shrub, planted in a single row, will make an informal hedge; those that can be clipped and will survive to make a formal hedge are far less common; those that can be clipped and will survive salt laden gales are very few in number.

As with shelter belts, good soil preparation and the removal of perennial weeds, the use of young plants and keeping them weed free all contribute to the early and successful establishment of hedges. When possible planting a hedge against small mesh wire netting or similar screening encourages more rapid and upright growth. Weeds compete for food and water, so reducing the rate of growth, and what is worse may smother the lower branches and leave them permanently bare. A single row of hedge plants is easier to keep weed free and double rows have no real advantage.

Fig. 2. The distinctive leaves of Cordyline australis 'Purpurea'.

Most of the suitable shrubs may be planted 1 foot to 3 feet (0.3-0.9m) apart and, except for those intended to form single stems, are best hard pruned after the first year of growth. This will involve the removal of at least half of the leading upright shoots and trimming the more or less horizontal shoots to leave them 6 to 8 inches long (15-20cm). This will encourage a good thick bottom to the hedge and, as the seasons pass, the trimming should be designed to produce a broad base and narrow top. Such a shape not only tends to preserve the lower branches because they receive more light than when the sides are vertical or undercut, it also reduces the risk of the tops being broken in heavy snow. With the bottom forming a solid barrier and the top a permeable one, such a hedge makes an almost ideal type of low windbreak with good protection at ground level and a filtering top that reduces wind turbulence.

The range of seaside shrubs to consider for hedges is greater than for trees for shelter belts but they are still few in comparison with those that may be planted inland.

Escallonia. This genus from the shores of South America contains some of the best seaside hedges. *E. macrantha* and the two Cornish cultivars 'Crimson Spire' and 'Red Hedger' are wind and salt tolerant and fairly frost hardy. Many of the others are too flimsy or slow growing, straggling and less frost hardy. The cheapest method of forming a hedge of these plants is by preparing the strip of ground for the hedge early in the autumn and inserting cuttings in a single row from mid-October onwards. The cuttings, of current years growth up to 12 inches (30cm) long, and inserted at least two thirds of their length in the soil at a foot apart (30cm), will root by the spring and make some growth in the summer. Plants raised from cuttings rooted elsewhere may suffer a little in the move but may be pruned after planting in the early spring.

Escallonias may be clipped twice or more each year, when they will make solid hedges rivalling close clipped yew or privet in appearance. Clipped once a year in July these escallonias make short growths before the winter which then carry a striking display of red flowers in spring and early summer. They may be 'burnt' by equinoxal gales and lose many of their leaves in the coldest winters but recover next spring and are among the best of shrubs for seaside hedges.

Elaeagnus. Several of the evergreen species and their cultivars are even hardier than the escallonias but are less easily propagated and slower growing. *E.* × *ebbingei, E. pungens* and some of its variegated forms are among the best for use as hedges. They may be trimmed with shears once a year in July or pruned with secateurs to a less formal shape. *E.* × *reflexa* may also be used and has the additional value of producing scandent branches that will scramble up into older shelter belts to fill the gaps at their base if planted close enough to the trees.

Olearia. Some of these New Zealand shrubs with small daisy-like flowers make useful hedges in the milder districts but are mostly better when untrimmed and spreading. *O.* × *haastii* is the hardiest and thrives inland in the north of England but is not very tall nor quick growing. It can be made into a neat formal hedge up to about 5 feet tall (1.5m) almost anywhere. *O. macrodonta* with grey holly like leaves and broad panicles of small white flowers in June-July, can make an informal hedge up to 15 feet (4.5m) but is less satisfactory when close trimmed. It has been killed to the ground in the coldest winters but usually springs again from the base. *O. virgata* behaves in the same way but makes even more rapid growth, in one instance reaching 12 feet (3.6m) three years after a very sharp frost had killed all the top growth. This shrub has somewhat rosemary-like leaves and upright growth that withstands the most severe gales.

Even faster growing is *O. traversii* but it is even less frost hardy and has been killed except where growing very close to the sea. It is so quick growing that its roots rarely keep it erect in the early years except when strongly staked or hard pruned to reduce the imbalance of top and root growth. Even so, planted young, against good artificial shelter or strong

Fig. 3. The dwarf fan palm, Chamaerops humilis.

stakes and with half its annual growth removed in each of the first three years, it is one of the best hedges for seaside gardens in the mildest areas.

Several other olearias, such as *O. albida, O. avicennifolia, O. paniculata,* with leaves rather like *Pittosporum tenuifolium,* and *O. solandri,* looking rather like a tall golden leaved heather, may be used as hedges in suitable climates.

Senecio rotundifolius, now more correctly known as *S. reinholdii,* has some of the toughest leathery evergreen leaves of any New Zealand shrub but is better when allowed to spread than when trimmed. It has succumbed to frost in recent years.

Euonymus japonicus is mostly undamaged by the worst gales and is frost hardy in most parts of the country, the exception being in the mildest places where it makes new soft growth in autumn that may be killed by sharp frosts in the winter. It is however a most useful hedge plant for seaside gardens.

The tamarisks are well known seaside shrubs, wind hardy and frost resistant, that provide useful permeable shelter. They have been trimmed to make formal hedges but do not survive long in that condition. There are several species; *Tamarix anglica,* often included in *T. gallica,* being regarded as denizens or established species in this country, and *T. parviflora, T. pentandra* and *T. tetrandra* from southern Europe and western Africa, will all serve well as informal screens or even thrive in the outer defences with the commoner natives.

Other shrubs that may be considered as shelter hedges in certain conditions include *Griselinia littoralis* that can be transplanted as quite large shrubs and are particularly suitable for growing in the semi-shade of failing shelter belts and will slowly make useful hedges in the mildest climates. *Fuchsia magellanica* 'Riccartonii' makes an attractive flowering hedge in mild seaside districts, it will often reach 6 feet (1.8m) and has been known to double that height in the absence of sharp frosts. Even if cut to the ground it survives in all but the coldest parts of the country. *Muehlenbeckia complexa,* sometimes known as the wirenetting plant, has very thin wiry stems that will scramble upwards through and over any plant or fence, and quickly makes an almost impenetrable mass of twining shoots in milder districts. Some of the hebes are sufficiently wind resistant to be useful as dwarf hedges near the coast and several pittosporums are useful as tall screens in the mildest districts.

Artificial shelter
Walls and stone-faced banks make permanent boundaries and provide solid shelter that can be a useful start in providing maximum shelter for seaside gardens. Wooden fences of various kinds, wire and plastic netting and various plastic fences all make temporary screens against which hedge shrubs can grow to useful heights. Whatever is chosen it is of the greatest importance that the stakes and other supports are adequate. A fence that provides useful shelter throughout the year and is then blown down in the strongest gale is worse than useless. For without shelter suitable plants will grow dwarf and compact and survive even the worst gales. Within sheltered gardens the same plants will grow taller and more open and then be damaged if shelter is removed. So stout posts, deeply set in the ground, supporting struts or wires all strongly held

Fig. 4. The creamy white flower spikes of Yucca gloriosa.

together by strong screws, nails and wire if any fence is to be held up in the occasional hurricane. Remember too that gales often bring rain and the additional weight of water makes most fences even heavier and more difficult to support.

Windswept gardens

Before the shelter is established, or even without it, some gardeners rely only on wind hardy plants to form the framework of their gardens. Such gardens can be economical of time and energy, requiring little pruning, clipping, staking or tying, but they lack many well-loved features of other gardens. They can be open and sunny on calm bright days and allow maximum advantage of any distant views but are not tempting to work, recreation or armchair relaxation when the winds blow. In due course odd sheltered corners are created but they will generally lack the calm of more sheltered gardens. Such windswept gardens left without the addition of shelter are quite unsuitable for most of the herbaceous plants; many annuals and bedding plants are susceptible to sudden winds and fruit and vegetable gardens may be impossible.

Those who would eschew shelter for gardens by the sea must rely on the trees and shrubs already suggested for use as shelter with the addition of others that may thrive in such conditions without providing shelter. In large gardens this will mean that specimens or small groups of the few trees suggested will have to be the main feature with other specimens and groups of wind hardy shrubs. Smaller gardens can be largely planted with these shrubs, in borders or as groups or specimens in lawns or longer grass.

There are other trees and shrubs, unsuitable as windbreaks, that can be added to those mentioned. They can provide variety of form and colour and produce a distinctive type of garden, particularly in the milder counties. Among them is *Cordyline australis,* often known as dracaena, which grows to 15 or 20 feet (4.5-6m), with one or more bare trunks topped with clusters of long strap shaped pointed leaves. The older leaves die and hang down beneath the green leaves to form a somewhat untidy bunch at the head of each stem. From this bunch there usually emerges each early summer a strong panicle of heavily scented creamy white flowers. These flower stalks are best removed after the flowers die in order to improve the appearance and reduce the weight at the top of the plant. Not everyone approves of the shape and often bedraggled appearance of *Cordyline* but it provides a distinctive feature of many seaside gardens.

The other similar trees usually grouped as palms are liable to be even more damaged by salty gales but where they grow they demonstrate the mildness of the garden and must be considered for inclusion in any seaside plot. *Trachycarpus fortunei,* the Chusan palm, grows tall over the years on rather thin single stems, covered with the rough hairy remains of old leaf stalks. These slow growing stems are topped by clusters of palm shaped leaves and carry yellowish flowers each summer. *Chamaerops humilis,* the dwarf fan palm, is the only European native palm but is less hardy than the Chusan. It has many similar leaves and

Fig. 5. Yucca filamentosa variegata.

flowers but even slower growing stems. Both are better when well sheltered but in exposed gardens provide distinctive features, although tattered and torn.

In the mildest gardens one or two agaves may be used to provide other distinctive shapes with their rosettes of sharp pointed, tough succulent leaves. *Agave parryi* is the hardiest and *A. americana* the largest and most exciting. These grow steadily for many years, the latter is known rather extravagantly as the century plant, and then each sends up a single stem 10 feet (9m) or more in height with numerous cream-coloured flowers for much of its length. Each plant then dies but may leave offsets to continue the vegetative phase. Similar outlines are given by the several species of *Yucca* with clusters of pointed leaves. Some species have stems carrying the leaves upwards, others develop several rosettes at ground level. All produce tall stems bearing whitish lily-like flowers which add to their attraction. In full exposure to sun and wind, on well-drained soils, these plants will thrive in quite cold climates.

More tender but even more striking is the Mexican *Beschorneria yuccoides* which grows with similar rosettes of pointed leaves. It is perennial and, facing south, it throws rapidly growing rose pink stems upwards to 8 feet (2·4m). All the bracts on these stems have a similar pink colour but, contrariwise, the small flowers are bright green.

With these spiky monocotyledonous plants to provide contrast and distinction may be associated the pampas grass *Cortaderia selloana* and its several varieties. Once established in a lawn or alone in a bed it will remain as a bold mass of leaves to produce the large plume of flowers in late summer.

To turn from the spiky plants among the wind resistant hardy shrubs and trees we can find many others that will thrive but have little value as shelter.

Among them must be included the large and increasingly popular heathers. Many, particularly the dwarf species of *Erica, Calluna* and *Daboecia,* originate in exposed areas and will give long periods of interest with a range of colours with their white, pink and purple flowers and foliage from pale yellow through many greens to deepest purple. The possibilities are extensive and most will do well in exposed conditions. The exceptions are the taller species that may be broken and bent but *E. arborea alpina, E. mediterranea* and *E. lusitanica* can by judicious early pruning be built up into useful plants even in quite windy conditions. The removal of half the length of last year's shoots after flowering reduces the amount exposed to the wind and allows a good root system to be established.

There are also many more escallonias, hebes and olearias than those most suitable as shelter hedges that can be grown for decorative effect in windy gardens. Among the escallonias 'Apple Blossom' and its several dwarf relations, the tall growing 'C.F. Ball' and the cascade forms 'Donard Seedling' and 'Langleyensis' are all attractive shrubs. The long spiked hebes have a wide range of colours from white through pale pink to purple to deep red. 'Alicia Amherst', 'Miss E. Fittall', 'Purple Queen' and 'Simon Deleaux' are among the best. *Olearia* × *scilloniensis*

Fig. 6. Agave americana.

smothers itself with the purest white flowers every spring, the Splendens hybrids produce similar masses of pink, blue and mauve michaelmas-daisy-like flowers and *Olearia semi-dentata* has individual flowers of mauve colour some 2 inches across (5cm). Similarly the several variegated elaeagnus, dwarf senecios and such compact shrubs as *Genista hispanica,* the Spanish gorse, *Ulex europaeus* 'Plenus', the double native gorse, and *Cassinia leptophylla.* Many of the species and forms of cistus grow well if planted young and small, but when they become larger they are susceptible to branch breaking by wind.

Even smaller and close to the ground the rock roses, *Helianthemum,* and dwarf osteospermums *(Dimorphotheca)* will provide good ground cover that is but little disturbed by wind. In the mildest parts the half-hardy gazanias can be equally useful.

All the dwarf bulbs, such as snowdrops, crocus, miniature daffodils and the smaller so-called botanical tulips and many less common small bulbs, such as iris, scilla, erythronium, ipheon, nerine, schizostylis and tigridia can be tucked away between shrubs and other plants. An exposed garden can thus be designed to grow compact, attractive plants to flower throughout the year and requiring no excessive amount of attention. Such gardens, exposed to the sea breezes, would have the trees or shrubs we have mentioned according to size. Planted in borders or island beds, with the slower growing plants as initial ground cover and provide interest while the larger specimens are growing to fill the space provided. Mown lawns or rough grass will give access and foreground to such features. Mostly rounded in shape the trees and shrubs must be relieved by some of the erect or spiky plants we have noticed and if more detail is needed the small bulbs and, perhaps very dwarf annuals sown in gaps in the ground cover could be added at will.

These exposed gardens that we have just envisaged might gradually provide sheltered corners where more delicate plants will thrive but will not allow many other forms of gardening for which shelter is essential. The exception is the rock garden if the low growing plants are selected. A rock bank or separate rockery or naturally stony or rocky part of the garden can be planted with a wide range of plants that will cover the stones and cling to the ground with little to fear from the worst gales. They do, however, increase the demand for weeding and tidying although, as in all windswept gardens, the removal by picking or sweeping of autumn leaves is rarely necessary as a gale of wind can usually be relied on to pick them up and swirl them away perhaps beyond sight or perhaps where they can be picked up and carried to the compost heap.

Turning now from the windswept gardens to those that are more sheltered let us consider the opportunities. This shelter may come from the natural situation as a hollow among rolling hills or the shelter belts and hedges we discussed on earlier pages.

Apart from the wind the other main factor that will limit the type of gardening will be the soil. As in any garden, chalk down, limestones and most blown sea sands will usually limit ornamental gardening to plants that will grow in alkaline conditions. This eliminates camellias, rhododendrons and other ericaceous shrubs. Some of the more acid soils that are suitable for these shrubs may have the disadvantage of being shallow over solid rock or containing much broken stone in the surface layer that makes cultivation difficult. This feature is not restricted to the seaside but it is a problem there as many shelter plants and others are less

Fig. 7. Map to demonstrate the mild climate enjoyed by many coastal regions.

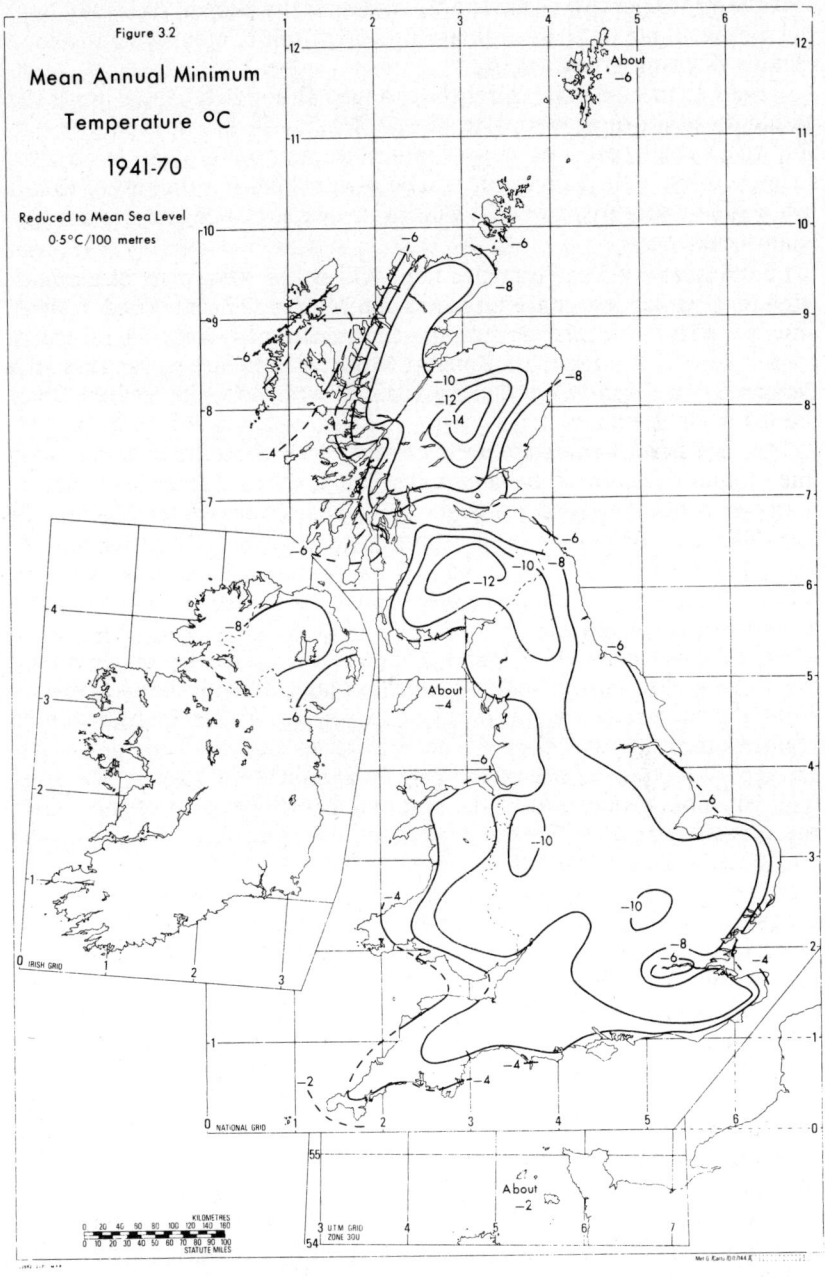

21

likely to remain upright without the good anchorage of deep roots in deep soils.

If the site is flat beside an estuary or marsh the alluvial soils may have the disadvantage of poor drainage or a high salt content which follows regular flooding at high tides.

Whatever the soil it can rarely be changed although it can be improved within the limits of its type. The wise gardeners will choose their plants to suit the conditions. For enthusiasts with a special plant hobby the struggle to grow their favourite will be worthwhile. For the rest of us it is more satisfactory to grow what will, to row with the tide and not struggle against adversity.

In almost every seaside garden there will be the advantage of a milder climate, in which less common plants can be tried. This may be a relative advantage to be compared with similar conditions inland. The Cornish south coast is milder than Bodmin Moor, the Sussex coast than the Downs or Weald and even the east coast, if well sheltered, less cold than the wolds or Pennines.

This is where the seaside gardener will seek the reward of growing more unusual shrubs, bulbs and other plants. Often they will survive for many years but then succumb to the occasional severe winter. Then, as in 1946/47, 1962/63 and 1981/82, short sharp frosts kill or badly damage many half-hardy plants that seem to be more susceptible because of the long mild autumns that encourage growth to continue, and delay the ripening of the wood.

Here the gardener has to decide, when starting a garden or replanting one after a devastating frost, whether to play safe with hardy plants or enjoy the colour, shape and rarity of tender plants that may have to be replaced in a few years time. The half-hardy acacias, hebes, olearias, scented rhododendrons and the early magnolias are all very tempting and, for most people, worth the cost and effort of replacing them after the occasional losses. Similarly agapanthus, gazanias, osteospermums and other low growing plants provide bright summer colours and are worth the trouble of replacing every few years or of taking 'insurance cuttings' each autumn to hold under glass and survive the frosts. Gardens planned to grow these and other typical seaside plants will need the shelter we have discussed and will be best if planted also with groups of hardier plants so that the garden will not be entirely spoilt by losses in hard winters.

What, now, of the orthodox gardener, if such there be, or he who has gardened inland and wishes to continue on the same lines? Let us look at the possibilities.

There are always limitations, for even with massive shelter, penetrating winds can still cause occasional damage so that some plants are unsuitable. Most of the tall herbaceous plants, such as delphiniums and hollyhocks, that are costly to stake anyway, are rarely worth

Fig. 8. Logan gardens, Ardwell, Dumfries and Galloway. A fine example of a garden with an exceptionally mild climate.

planting by the sea. Sweet peas are liable to be blown to pieces sometime during the season. Roses tend to be difficult because the moist atmosphere encourages black spot disease and the mild winters encourage almost perennial growth. The disease can be kept in check by regular spraying. The weakening effects of the long winter growth can be overcome by cutting back tall shoots in the autumn followed by proper pruning in early spring: generous feeding with a rose fertilizer in the growing season will also help to keep the plants vigorous.

Good dahlias are grown near the sea but they need shelter, more than usually strong staking and tying and the sunniest possible position to avoid the grey mould which comes in moist conditions. For any but the exhibitor dahlia roots can often be left in the ground year after year in the milder districts.

Some trees and shrubs dislike both wind and wet and in most seaside gardens the tolerant are to be recommended (see pp. 24-27).

Apples and pears are very difficult to grow to perfection because broken branches spoil the shape of the trees and allow disease entry through the wounds, while the damp conditions favour canker and scab that are among the most serious disorders. But fruit for home use only can be produced.

In the vegetable garden some special precautions are necessary and some modifications of methods will give better results (see pp. 33-35).

These limitations will not deter some enthusiasts who will do anything to grow their favourite plants, by altering the soil conditions, regular spraying against pests and diseases, providing ample shelter and solid staking and tying. If that is the intention then these steps must be taken adequately and in full knowledge of the problems. Others will accept the conditions and turn for their gardening enjoyment to the plants that will thrive without extra attention.

Shrubs

Borders and beds of shrubs among lawns or grass, or other paths, can be attractive at all seasons and are the least labour demanding of garden plants.

Most of the shrubs recommended as sheltering hedges are equally useful for ornament. Untrimmed some may make substantial plants but those carefully cut back to prevent encroachment on others can remain attractive and will flower.

Most escallonias produce a wealth of flowers during the late spring and through the summer. The shorter cultivars such as 'Apple Blossom', 'Peach Blossom', 'Donard Radiance' and 'Donard Star' almost cover themselves with pink or red flowers for several weeks every summer. They need little pruning other than the removal of the most heavily flowered branches on which there are no shoots for next year's flowering or a branch that is sticking out in the wrong direction. Others, such as *E. fonkii,* 'Edinensis', 'Langleyensis' and 'Donard Seedling', make taller bushes up to 8 feet in height (2.4m) with most of their flowers on hanging branches produced during the previous summer; these should be removed after flowering.

The olearias are also summer flowering, mostly with small white daisy-like flowers, some of which have a sweet scent. The exceptions are the Splendens group with blue, mauve and pink flowers in the spring. *O.* × *scilloniensis* also flowers early and has the purest white flowers of any, that often completely cover the plants. Probably the most striking is the mauve flowered *O. semidentata,* with single blooms an inch or more across (2.5cm). Not very hardy but worth a place in any mild seaside garden.

Olearia paniculata (once known as *O. forsteri*) is another less hardy species but its neat shape, pale leaves with undulating edges and tiny sweetly scented flowers in late summer make it worthy of a place in any

Fig. 9. Pittosporum tenuifolium; an attractive shrub that grows well in milder gardens.

seaside garden even if only for a few years before a rare frost kills it. Similarly *O. solandri,* with its almost golden heath-like leaves, should also be included.

Elaeagnus are rarely grown for their flowers or occasional fruit but for their leaves and they are often in demand by the flower arrangers. In particular the several variegated forms of *E. pungens* although the evergreen *E.* × *ebbingei* and *E. maculata* are attractive with pale backs to their leaves and are as hardy as any of the typical seaside shrubs.

The heathers, *Calluna, Daboecia* and *Erica,* all grow well in exposed positions although some of the taller exotic species may need heading back for a year or two while good root systems are established. Some, such as *E. lusitanica* are not quite so hardy as the numerous forms of our natives but they and other taller species can be used with good effect among heathers in most seaside situations.

Pittosporum tenuifolium in its several forms grows well in milder gardens. They can be damaged by strong winds and are best grown within a sheltered area if the attractive foliage is to be usable for cutting. It is not always realised that they and most other half-hardy species have strongly scented flowers usually in the spring of the year. The larger leaved *P. eugenioides* and its variegated form make attractive bushes that survive most winters in the south-west.

In addition to olearias there are other shrubs with daisy-like flowers that withstand most strong winds. One of the toughest in exposed positions is *Senecio reinoldii,* a large shrub formerly known by the more descriptive name of *S. rotundifolius.* Many specimens had survived close to the sea until the winter of 1978/79 and would probably give many more years of service if planted again. The smaller species *S. greyii, S. hectorii, S.* 'Sunshine' and *S. monroi,* are useful squat evergreen shrubs with annual displays of bright yellow flowers.

Dry, well-drained soils suit the Mediterranean cistuses and their relations *Halimium,* the hybrid × *Halimiocistus* and *Helianthemum.* In full sun all bear a fleeting but long succession of flowers in white, yellow, pink, red and mauve through the summer months. If planted when small they adapt themselves to windy situations and helianthemums can be clipped after flowering to maintain their compact habit. The others are less tolerant of cutting but some pruning is needed occasionally to keep them in shape. Cistus in particular provide the warm tang of the Mediterranean when the sun shines on them in British gardens.

Many other shrubs successfully grown in inland gardens can also thrive in shelter by the sea and new seaside gardeners may wish to introduce cherished favourites from former gardens. But in milder districts so many less common plants can be grown that there is little space and less inducement to include the commoner plants. The exceptions, on acid soils in the higher rainfall districts with more frequent moist days and nights, are the innumerable species of rhododendron and their extensive range of hybrids and cultivars. From the creeping *R. repens* to the tree-like *R. arboreum,* large-leaved *R. grande* and the slightly tender Loderi hybrids, they are all better in the light shade of oak or similar woodlands. Shelter from wind is also important for most of them, even the common *R. ponticum* is burnt by salt-laden gales but the combined influence of higher humidity and lower

Fig. 10. The daisy-like, yellow flowers of Senecio 'Sunshine'.

frost risk should encourage many seaside gardeners who have shelter and an acid soil to consider the rhododendrons.

The same is true of the increasingly popular camellias. They also dislike lime or chalk in the soil and many thrive in partial shade but while they will not stand salt spray many will grow well in drier sunnier conditions than most rhododendrons.

Fig. 11. Abutilon megapotamicum, an attractive climber for a sunny wall.

Climbers

Walls and fences near the coast offer temptation to experiment with tender climbing plants. The fast-growing *Rosa banksiae* and its white variety will survive in mild districts and quickly smother the largest walls in a very short time if provided with supporting wires or trellis. *Solanum crispum* and *S. jasminoides* will also flourish although damp summer days may bring the unpleasant smell of potato blight disease to the more leafy *S. crispum*. *Lapageria rosea* grows well on north walls in the mildest places. It may be cut down in the coldest winters but growing from beneath dwarf shrubs the roots survive and with ample organic manuring and generous watering will soon return to considerable height if support is available. The various shades of pink bell-like flowers appear in the late summer and go on well into the autumn.

Several jasmines and honeysuckles flower well over long periods. In addition to *Jasminum nudiflorum,* the hardy winter species, which has

Fig. 12. The variegated foliage of Actinidia kolomikta.

more opportunity of showing its yellow flowers without damage, the various forms of *J. officinale* and *J. polyanthum* are worth placing against warm south-facing walls. By planting a number of different species of the climbing loniceras the scent of honeysuckle can be obtained through much of the year.

The actinidias also make useful wall coverings. *A. kolomikta,* with variegated foliage, and *A. chinensis* with its edible fruit, are both suitable for sunny walls. The latter, now sold in fruiterers' shops as kiwi fruit, regularly produce crops along the south coast.

There are several other plants, better known in temperate greenhouses inland, that can be used on sunny walls in milder districts. *Abutilon megapotamicum,* the shrubby acacias, *Clianthus puniceus,* some cestrums, the passion flower, *Passiflora caerulea* and *Sollya heterophylla* are among the colourful and unusual shapes that are worth trying in these situations.

Bamboos

Several of this large related group of giant grasses can be used to provide protection from wind and to give distinctive shape and form, particularly in the larger seaside gardens. As shelter plants they tend to look rather tattered by the end of the winter but another growth of the annual stems will set them up for their summer display. Within the protection of other shelter and with some shade they provide distinctive outlines of evergreen leaves that break the solidity that is so often presented by many wind-hardy shrubs.

Arundinaria japonica is the most common and probably the hardiest bamboo but none the less valuable for that. *A. nitida* has smaller leaves and is not quite so tall but tends to spread rather more when well established in suitable conditions. *A. pumila* and *A. pygmaea* are much smaller, the first about 2 to 3 feet (60-90cm) and the latter less than a foot (30cm) but both spread quickly and for that reason need careful placing if they are to be planted. There are many more of greater height that can be used in suitable conditions. Most of them thrive best in moist organic soil and light shade.

Conifers

Many of this group of trees also provide perpendicular lines among more stolid plants, for instance the smaller junipers and cypresses among heathers and other small shrubs, or taller chamaecyparis and cypresses among larger trees and shrubs. The horizontal branches of cedars, firs and spruces provide alternative and different lines where space is not limited. Except for the few described among the plants for shelter most are damaged by wind and salt and are best placed within the shelter of tougher trees and shrubs.

Bulbs and Corms

In addition to the many hardy bulbs that provide colour in grass or among shrubs and herbaceous plants there are several bulbs and corms that can be grown in the milder seaside gardens. Most of them are at their best where the soil is light and dries out in the summer. *Amaryllis belladonna,* the crinums and their hybrids, the several agapanthus and many alliums all thrive in such conditions. Tulips and gladioli, particularly the smaller species and hybrids of each, will continue to grow for many years without being lifted annually as they need to be in damp cool conditions. The less hardy tazetta narcissus, tigridia, ixia and sparaxis all add colour to spring and summer gardens while the Kaffir lily, *Schizostylis coccinea,* and its pink and red flowered cultivars do the same in late summer and long into the autumn. *Crocosmia* and its near relation *Curtonus,* some of which are still known by the old name of montbretia, are also useful in the late summer and autumn.

Fig. 13. The unusual yellow flowers of Tigridia pavonia, a bulbous species that blooms in late summer.

Herbaceous plants

Lack of time or gardening help makes it difficult to grow any plant that needs staking or tying. In seaside gardens the menace of frequent strong winds makes it even more important to choose sturdy plants that will stand erect without the aid of sticks or string. There are several that are available and some have become well known in the milder gardens. Acanthus, with their striking spiny perennial leaves and spikes of distinctive flowers rising to 5 feet or more (1.5m) are especially useful. The wand flowers *Dierama pulcherrima,* ranging in colour through the pinks, reds and purples and in height from 2 to 6 feet (60cm to 1.8m), although seemingly fragile will stand alone and add interest to many gardens in July and August.

Day lilies or hemerocallis now have a wider range of colour in the reds, yellows and oranges and of shape than formerly and, with many flowers on each stem, the transient flowers are regularly replaced to provide a show over a long period in the summer. Their long curving leaves are alone also attractive in the spring and after the flower stems have been removed in the autumn.

Cortaderia selloana, the pampas grass, can form a massive feature in a garden of sufficient size either as a single plant in a lawn or at the back of a large border. The pale rough leaves may be scorched by the gales but new ones grow each year and the white plumes will grow to 7 or 8 feet tall (2.1 to 2.4m) and remain erect in all but the strongest gales.

There are many species and cultivars of *Kniphofia,* mostly known as red hot pokers or torch lilies. Among them can be found colourful plants that will flower from early summer to mid-autumn, while their long leaves cover the ground for the whole year.

Such perennial-leaved plants as are mentioned above have this advantage of ground cover which smothers weeds and reduces the need for hoeing. The more usual herbaceous plants have perennial roots but lose their leaves in the winter and thus allow weeds to grow in the milder winters. Many are susceptible to slugs and snails, the bane of gardeners in mild damp districts and the tallest, such as the delphiniums, lupins, eremurus and phlox are also so easily damaged by wind as to be not worth attempting.

Ground cover has become a popular concept in recent years and has been well covered in No 26 of this series of handbooks. For seaside gardeners there are the usual requirements of starting with ground free of perennial weeds and choosing plants to suit the soil and climatic conditions. Being mostly low growing the usual ground cover plants are unlikely to be bothered by even the strongest gales but salt, borne by onshore winds, may damage some plants. A few species are established as typical ground covering plants in the milder climates. The mesembryanthemums, now divided into several genera, with fleshy leaves and yellow, pink, red or mauve flowers grow well and will cover rocks or in poor soil. Where conditions suit them they can be well used at the seaside.

Other South Africans with low growing habits are similarly useful but are also liable to be lost in cold spells. The osteospermums, formerly *Dimorphotheca,* cover the ground quite quickly and *O. barbarae, O. caulescens, O. ecklonis* and their hybrids will survive most winters in the mild districts. Gazanias too produce attractive cover and a long succession of daisy-like flowers. Both gazanias and osteospermums are easily propagated and by taking a few cuttings each autumn and keeping them under cover they can be maintained even if the parents are killed when left in the open.

Erigeron glaucus, another trailer with plenty of large pinkish mauve daisy flowers, must have dry conditions and ample sun if it is to thrive but is an easy plant to grow in such conditions.

Fig. 14. A clump of Kniphofia 'Royal Standard' growing by the sea.

Here, as with many other plants, there are other low growing plants that will grow in suitable conditions but the few mentioned are among the best for use as low cover in the milder seaside districts.

Vegetables
The pleasures of eating fresh home-grown vegetables and salads and even of stocking deep freeze cabinets or other stores are not diminished in seaside gardens. Almost all that is said in *The Vegetable Garden Displayed* applies to gardening by the sea. We will consider the special needs of the seaside vegetable gardener.

On many coasts valuable organic manure is there for the carting. Seaweed carried from the high tide mark or even cut from the rocks has been used for generations to manure nearby farms and gardens. It is heavy, unless allowed to dry which is difficult on public beaches. It now so often contains unwanted plastics and other undesirable debris that it is best sorted as it is collected to avoid cluttering the garden with unwanted and indestructible rubbish. An added disadvantage is the attraction of seaweed for flies that will then invade house and other buildings.

For this reason seaweed is best hauled in winter, when flies are less plentiful, and spread on uncropped land to be dug in when partially dried. It can also be most useful in assisting the decay of garden waste on

33

the compost heap. Mixed with weeds and other waste and covered with lawn mowings or leaves decay goes on apace and flies are discouraged.

On many shores the weed is mixed with broken shells that contain much calcium thus raising the pH of the material and making it unsuitable for application to acid-loving plants. It is however very welcome in the vegetable garden where the pH is always slowly dropping as calcium is leached from the soil.

Wind has already been mentioned! Some may say too often but it is an ever present problem and influences several vegetable garden practices. Unless the vegetable garden is fully sheltered runner beans will be difficult to keep erect on tall sticks and the field method of allowing them to run on the ground with their tips removed regularly, may be a better system. Similarly dwarf peas may be better than the taller cultivars on sticks or string.

It is often desirable to earth up the taller winter brassicas and brussels sprouts, sprouting and winter broccoli. The mildest districts allow regular cropping of winter cauliflower or broccoli from November to May in most years but they are better when the soil is well drained and the stems are supported by earthing the rows like potatoes.

It is rare that frost is so hard beside the sea that the usual vegetables will not overwinter but broad beans, sown in the autumn, can be so battered by wind and swirled around in muddy little holes that they die of drowning instead of frost. Later sowing under cloches for protection or under glass for planting out may be better in exposed positions. Winter lettuce and spring onions can also be blown to pieces when strong winds sweep across exposed gardens.

Cloches, frames and plastic tunnels are useful in any vegetable garden. In exposed positions they may be at risk and special precautions are necessary. The older glass cloches usually remain firm except in the teeth of the gales. It is a good plan however to draw a slight drill on each side of the row of cloches so that they settle more quickly into the soil and so remain firm. However tunnels of pliable plastic are not usually damaged unless a tear appears when the whole may then be ripped away.

In the same way an open door or ventilator on the windward side of a greenhouse will allow pressure to build up and blow out glass on the other side. Even the overlapping glass allows some air to penetrate and it has been found worthwhile to open ventilators on the lee side to reduce the pressure and the risk of damage.

The damp atmosphere in seaside gardens encourages potato blight disease earlier in the season and more regularly than in drier districts. (It also infects tomatoes.) Spraying to prevent attacks, whenever moist, misty conditions arrive and before the appearance of the disease, is essential for tomatoes even under glass if potatoes are growing nearby. Spraying may also be necessary for midseason and maincrop potatoes if they are grown although it is doubtful if they are worth growing in small

Fig. 15. Lapageria rosea, a climber for north walls in mild areas.

gardens. Earlies can be planted earlier and have their haulms cut off when blight begins to appear because unless spraying is thorough and frequent it is of little use in the mild wet days of a seaside summer.

Fruit
Most of the many valuable fruits that can be grown in English gardens are not at their best in seaside gardens. They can be grown, nothing is impossible in gardening, but they often cause more trouble than they are

worth or produce lower quality crops than can be expected inland.

New fruit trees, and others, are best planted very young. Older and larger ones will have great difficulty in producing an adequate root system to hold up the head of branches, leaves and fruits in windy conditions. Whatever the age adequate staking is essential in the first years and the stem or trunk must be wrapped to prevent chafing against ties and stakes.

Apple trees, bushes or trained cordons or espaliers are best pruned and trained by the gardener and not by the wind. Wind-shaped trees will produce fruit of sorts but unless shelter is provided fruit growing is hardly worth contemplating. If flowering coincides with strong winds the flight of pollinating insects will be reduced and less fruit set. If autumn gales come before ripening or picking time windfalls will be more plentiful. Even earlier the growing fruits may be damaged by being banged against each other and the rasp of leaves can damage the skin of the fruit. Worst of all the atmosphere near the sea is usually more humid and this encourages scab and canker. The former disease attacks leaves and twigs and spoils the appearance of fruit while canker kills twigs, branches and even whole trees. Both diseases can be controlled by spraying but it must be thorough and usually has to be more frequent in the moist conditions.

Brown rot also seems to be more troublesome in damp conditions and care needs to be taken to reduce or prevent it.

Pears present similar problems and really need even more attention almost everywhere in England if good quality fruit is to be grown.

Cherries and plums are equally liable to damage by wind and have somewhat similar diseases to those of the apple that are also encouraged by damp conditions. Heavy rain or a damp atmosphere at ripening time will encourage splitting of the fruit.

Peaches and nectarines really need the protection of walls with southerly aspects and they also need extra attention as to spraying and protection. The young shoots due to bear next year's fruit may be broken by the wind if not tied in as they grow. In very mild districts there will be insufficient low winter temperatures that are needed to break winter dormancy.

Walnuts are rarely planted nowadays but they dislike wind so are not suited to the seaside. Even the common hazel and its cultivated cousins the cob nuts and filberts need protection from wind at flowering time. If not sheltered the pollen from the catkins will be blown into the next parish and will not drop onto the tiny red female flowers that produce the nuts after pollination.

So it is not an encouraging outlook for the orchard fruit. Those who feel they must grow this 'top' fruit may either struggle to give all the attention that is necessary or they may give what shelter they can, plant their orchard and let it grow as it will. In this way some fruit will arrive in

Fig. 16. The passion flower, Passiflora caerulea; a climber for sunny walls.

due time, it will not be saleable or fit for shows but it still may be better than the 'Golden Delicious' apples or unripe 'Conference' pears in the shops.

As we have seen, the strong climber, *Actinidia chinensis,* will fruit in the milder areas and it may be possible to surprise ones friends with home-grown Chinese gooseberries or kiwi fruit as they are now named. On a wall or fence the supporting wires must be strong for the ample lengths of vine that this plant produces.

The soft, bush and cane fruits are more feasible given some shelter, although as with the larger fruit the greater dampness of seaside gardens can be a problem. Raspberries and red currants are particularly susceptible to wind damage; blackberries, loganberries, gooseberries and black currants are rather susceptible but all thrive best within good shelter. In all but the most exposed conditions strawberries are close enough to the ground to avoid serious damage. The uprights and wire on which some fruits are trained need to be rather stronger in windy situations as does the fruit cage which is essential if full crops of fruit are to be picked.

Strawberries, raspberries and loganberries are particularly susceptible to botrytis or grey mould in damp seaside climates and are also likely to increase in the shade cast by the hedges or screens needed to reduce wind damage. Spraying or dusting can help to reduce damage by mould and the selection of suitable varieties helps a little. Strawberries with smaller leaves and fruit standing above them such as 'Pantagruella' and raspberries such as 'Malling Jewel' and 'September' are likely to be slightly less affected than the more vigorous ones. 'September' fruits a little earlier than its name implies and than other autumn croppers. This usually allows some fruit to be picked before the damp autumn days make grey mould almost inevitable.

If loganberries are chosen the thornless clone is so much easier to handle than others and is a heavy cropper. The alternate training system where canes are tied into one side of the plant as they grow is better than allowing them to grow up over the fruiting area. In this way the fruit is left in the open and thus drier. Similarly the alternate cropping system for raspberries, where one row is cropped one year and the young canes removed to allow better growing and ripening conditions for the fruit can be more suitable in damp conditions.

Conclusion

Almost any plant can be grown in nearly any situation with the necessary money, time and skill to provide the right conditions. To go to extremes such as the commonly stated example of bananas at the North Pole is to invite continuous struggle, expenditure and frustration. At the other extreme the garden becomes a nature reserve and gardening is left to others. Gardening skills and knowledge from whatever source all assist in seaside gardening but it must again be emphasised that wind and moisture are the all-important limiting factors while the milder conditions brought by proximity to the sea is a bonus that allows some plants to be grown that need a greenhouse elsewhere.

Thus the seaside garden, of whatever size, shape or purpose, can be as varied as any other garden but with ample protection from wind, salt and driven sand, or with the plant inhabitants limited to those that withstand those enemies. In addition one can expect to find some truly exotic plants always being grown or attempted that are impossible in older gardens.

Appendix I

Further reading

Relatively few books have been published on this subject and the following list includes most of those written during the present century. Very few of them are still in print but some may be available in libraries.

Seaside planting of trees and shrubs, by A. Gaut (Country Life, 1907)
Sea-coast gardens and gardening, by F. A. Bardswell (Sherratt & Hughes, 1908)
Gardens near the sea, by Alice Launsherry (Stokes, New York, 1910)
Seaside planting for shelter, ornament and profit, by A. D. Webster (T. Fisher Unwin Ltd, 1918)
British & foreign trees and shrubs in Cornwall, by Edgar Thurston (Royal Institution of Cornwall; Cambridge University Press, 1930)
My garden by the sea, by R. A. Foster-Melliar (G. Bell & Sons Ltd, 1936)
Trees and shrubs for Cornwall, by J. W. Hunkin (Bishop of Truro), (CPRE and Royal Horticultural Society, c. 1947)
Shrubs for the milder counties, by W. Arnold-Forster (Country Life, 1948)

Fig. 17. Part of the garden at Tresco Abbey, Isles of Scilly. The Isles enjoy the mildest climate in the British Isles, due to their position off Cornwall and in the flow of the Gulf Stream.

Shelterbelts and Microclimate, by J. M. Caborn (Forestry Commission, HMSO 1957)
Seaside gardening, by C. Kelway (Collingridge, 1962)
Shelterbelts and windbreaks, by J. M. Caborn (Faber and Faber, 1965)
Gardening on sand, by C. Kelway (Collingridge, 1966)
Seaside plants of the world, by E. A. Menninger, DSc (Hearthside Press Inc., New York, 1966)
Gardening by the sea, by J. R. B. Evison (Pan Books, 1969)
Gardening on the coast, by C. Kelway (David & Charles, 1970)

The horticultural, meteorological and other scientific journals of the world contain numerous references to the subject of wind, its effect on plants and the methods of protecting them. Anyone wishing to study this subject in detail might well start by obtaining a copy of an annotated bibliography "The Response of Horticultural Crops to, and their protection from wind. 1960-65" from the Commonwealth Bureau of Horticulture and Plantation Crops, East Malling, Kent. That paper contains 89 references and if updated would, no doubt, contain many more.

Appendix II

A selection of gardens to visit. All the gardens listed below are situated on, or near, the coast, and many ideas can be gleaned from them. The opening times given were correct at the time of going to print but should always be checked in advance of a visit.

Many seaside resorts also have interesting gardens on the edge of the sea that demonstrate the value of shelter and the use of many of the plants discussed in this Handbook.

England
Abbotsbury Gardens, Abbotsbury, Dorset
Privately owned; open daily from March-September.

Compton Acres, Poole, Dorset
Privately owned; open daily Spring-Autumn.

Glendurgan, Mawnan Smith, Cornwall
National Trust; open fairly frequently Spring-Autumn. Many fine trees and shrubs flourish here in the mild Cornish climate.

Liverpool University Botanic Gardens, Ness, Neston, Merseyside
University of Liverpool; open throughout the year.

Sharpitor, Salcombe, Devon
National Trust; open throughout the year.

St Michael's Mount, Marazion, Cornwall
National Trust. Mount open daily during summer; garden open occasionally.

Trengwainton, Penzance, Cornwall
National Trust. Open regularly during the summer.

Channel Isles
La Colline, Jersey
Privately owned. Open most of the summer.

Isles of Scilly
Tresco Abbey, Tresco, Isles of Scilly
Privately owned; open all the year, except Sundays. A sub-tropical garden containing many fascinating plants.

Wales
Clyne Castle, Swansea, West Glamorgan
Swansea Corporation. Open throughout the year.

Plas Newydd, Isle of Anglesey, Gwynedd
National Trust; open daily (not Saturdays) Spring-Autumn. Peak season for the garden is in Spring.

Scotland
Achamore House, Isle of Gigha, Strathclyde
Privately owned. Open daily Spring-Autumn. An excellent example of the use of shelter belts.

Brodick Castle, Isle of Arran, Strathclyde
National Trust for Scotland. Open throughout the year.

Dunrobin Castle, Golspie, Highland
Privately owned. Open daily Spring-Autumn. Fine formal garden situated very near the sea.

Inverewe, Poolewe, Highland
National Trust for Scotland. Open throughout the year. One of the most famous coastal gardens in Europe, containing many rare plants.

Kiloran, Isle of Colonsay, Strathclyde
Privately owned. Open frequently throughout the year.

Logan, Ardwell, Dumfries and Galloway
Department of Agriculture and Fisheries for Scotland. Open daily April-September.